T0208668

I FOUND GRACE IN HIS SIGHT

Saved by His Grace

STABISO MADZIVA

authorHOUSE®

AuthorHouse™ UK Ltd.
500 Avebury Boulevard
Central Milton Keynes, MK9 2BE
www.authorhouse.co.uk
Phone: 08001974150

First published by AuthorHouse 5/11/2011

ISBN: 978-1-4567-7519-3 (sc)
ISBN: 978-1-4567-7520-9 (e)

PREFACE

They are not many times in life when you meet someone who according to the violations experienced in their life who still have so much love to give and who's mind is fixed on helping over's. Stabiso has endured the worst that this world could throw at her and she is still standing; not only standing but fighting back the best way possible by demonstrating love and giving hope to those who have or are experiencing similar torment by sharing her story. Star is by no means a perfect person but a person who has learnt from her mistakes and is willing to warn those who would listen to the dangers that lurk just around the corner.

My life has been touched and moved in hearing this tremendous testimony. Without Jesus in her life this story would not be possible. I hope that you will be equally move and inspired as you read.

DEDICATION

This book is dedicated with love to my partner and my four children who have stood by me and have been patient with me.

ACKNOWLEDGEMENT

First and foremost I would like to thank my Lord and saviour Jesus Christ for His grace that has brought me this far. I give Jesus Christ all the glory and honour for what He has done and will continue to do in my life.

I would like to thank Claudette Wray–Chambers who helped with the editing of this book. She has worked tirelessly and selflessly to help me finish this book. Thank you for showing me love, being patient, kind and understanding. Thank you for giving me your time when I knew you had a busy schedule.

I send a big thank you to Gift Muteletwa for helping me with the final touches and praying through the whole project. I appreciate you and this is only the beginning of greater things to come.

To Natasha my beautiful and talented daughter, thank you for designing the cover. May the Lord bless you my love.

I would also like to appreciate Pastor Andrew and his wife Lynne Spencer for being my spiritual parents and all the saints in my home church NDC. God bless you all and big love.

To my partner and all my children thank you for being a part of my life. I love you all.

To my Mum and Dad I love you, I appreciate and miss you.

Roda Madziva thank you for being the big sister I never had.

INTRODUCTION

It is my pleasure to introduce my readers to this book which tells a true story about my life, which on the one hand is a true account of how the devil can torment a life, while on the other conveying the message of love, in particular it is a life testimony of our Lord Jesus Christ as the deliverer (Psalms 22 v 2 NKJV), the founder of the lost (Luke 15 v 4, 24 NKJV) and the redeemer of mankind (Isaiah 63 v 18 or Psalms 19 v 14). It would have been a sad story or one not worth telling had it ended on the level of damage, and destruction which the devil has wrought in my life. In other words, this book would not be worth reading if the story of my life had only been based on how devastating the enemy can be. Instead, my life experiences, though not something I would have chosen had I been presented with a choice, have a happy ending.

My life story is one which speaks of the grace of our Lord Jesus Christ, in particular how He has delivered me from the enemy's destructive plan. On writing this book I felt fully convinced that the Lord was leading me along a path which I am certain will lead me to meet with my destiny. I also felt that the Holy Spirit was inspiring me to forewarn all the saints in whose hands this book will end up - for to be forewarned is to be forearmed.

As the church of God we should not be ignorant of Satan's devices. I believe that what I suffered in my childhood can be prevented from happening in the lives of many children. That is why I strongly feel that this book carries a message of deliverance which needs to be heard by every believer; both young and old.

CHAPTER 1

My name is Stabiso. I was born in a little village called Chiota in the town of Marondera in Zimbabwe. I was the seventh of nine children (that is until two of my brothers died). I was the first living girl born to my elderly parents, another girl was born after me but she died three days after birth. Then my mum had a boy and another girl after me.

Growing up in a village meant everyone around was related, I had my aunties and uncles all around us and we looked out for each other. However, there was always jealousy and malice amongst us and a lot of competition. If there was a good harvest there would be hatred but we as children had no control over that, we just grew up to the bickering of the elders. This hatred and jealousy could show itself in many ways, for example, on one occasion my family had a very good harvest of corn and a neighbor drove his cattle into our fields and destroyed the whole harvest. These actions had devastating impact each time they happened.

My dad worked as a builder and because of that he was away most of the time, my mum and my older brothers did all the farming on our small piece of land which we owned. I did not know we were poor because everyone I knew was the same and my dad had a big Chevrolet which we never rode in. I remember my siblings and I were really excited to see dad when he came home and we used to run to the gate which was at the perimeter of our smallholding to open it for him and then we would chase the car all the way home. When we got to the house, dad would always have sweets for us which he had brought back with him.

I did not have a bad childhood as such because we had each other. My siblings and I were grateful for the little we had and always managed to see the funny side of every situation. However, my happy childhood didn't last for long. One fateful day I had an encounter that was to shatter my innocence and change my life completely.

It all began in February 1980, at the time my mum had just been offered a chance to train as a village health worker in a neighboring township. As this was about 25 miles away from our home, it was not possible for her to travel home every day and she had to stay at the training school and only returned home at weekends. My brother Davis had to take care of us, he did the cooking and looked after my little sister, who was still very young when mum left, while I washed up, fetched water and hewed firewood. My other brothers, Given and Shabba looked after our cattle so I had to take some food to them every so often. I liked doing this because on my way to the veldts I got to pick and eat lots of wild fruits. It also gave me opportunity to look for firewood to take back home.

On my way back from the veldts one day, I was very thirsty and saw a bunch of sugarcane in a field of a neighbor, who was also a family member. I climbed over the fence, bruising my leg in the process and plucked some of the juicy sugarcane. Whilst I was feasting on my loot, the neighbor caught me and said "Come here you little thief". His voice was menacing. All my joy vanished as I knew I was in trouble; he pulled me by my arms and dragged me into a waterhole. The next thing I knew, his hands were inside my panties, "this is what you deserve", he said in his menacing voice. I tried to scream and he grabbed my mouth, and said if I made any noise he would throw me into the water.

He was smelly (a smell which even today comes back to me when I find myself in an atmosphere where I feel a little scared or uncomfortable), and he forced himself on me. That was the most painful experience of my life in my six years of life. When he had finished he pushed me up out of the well and told me to go home and said that if I told anyone about what had happened he would kill me and throw me in the well.

I was scared, I looked at my legs and I was bleeding. I was aching all over and could not even walk properly. I was scared to meet anyone in case they asked what was wrong with me, so I decided to hide and disappear from home. Unfortunately, that was the day my mum came back for the weekend from the training school. I did not know where to go so I decided to hide in the cornfield. I could hear my mum calling me but I stayed put until it was dark.

My mum organized a search party of family and friends and while they were looking for me, I ran inside the house and changed my clothes, and I made my appearance. That was my first secret and the end of my innocence. My mum was happy to see me, she did not notice anything in the dark and because of my disappearance, and they were more concerned about finding out from me why I couldn't hear when they were calling out to me.

My parents were good parents but very strict, I realized at an early age that there were things that you just don't talk about. To a six year old, telling my mum what had happened was something I knew I could never do because my abuser was a well respected member of our family. I knew that no one would ever believe me if anything, I would get beaten up for saying things like that. It was hard for me to keep this secret and to make matters worse, whenever I saw his children I wondered if he treated them the same. I began to withdraw into myself living in a dream world where that kind of thing never happened.

My family were very good farmers and because my dad was a builder, we only saw him in the night or during weekends. My brothers and my mum did all the work in the field. Unfortunately I was the first girl and because of that, I had to learn to do all the housework from an early age. We had time to play but it was limited. After school we had to do our work before we could play.

As I was growing up the boys were always in trouble with my dad for one thing or the other, my dad was a hard man to please. He pushed the boys so hard that one of my brothers left home and went to join the army at 16 years of age and we have never heard of him since, no one knows whether he is dead or alive. The war ended in 1980 when we got our independence but my brother did not come back and we never got to see his grave. My other brother went to join my uncle who worked in the mines that just put pressure on the ones that remained.

CHAPTER 2

My grandfather died in 1982 and we left the village for the capital city Harare. My parents sold the place we had in the village and combined the money with my other uncle who sold his house in the suburb area of Harare and together they bought a farm in Glenforest. I can say my life totally changed for the better. I had a bedroom to myself, we had electricity in the house, mum got a job as a nurse-aid at a nearby clinic and we had a helper named Josie who looked after us while mum was at work. We had a good life then though Josie used to bully me a lot and make me do her work.

We lived at this house with my uncle who was a Preacher and a business man and his four sons, his wife had just died of a heart attack. I really liked my uncle because he had time for us which we never had with our own dad. He would play his guitar to us and teach us some gospel songs; those were the best times we ever had with the whole family. My dad stopped working then, and he and my uncle started a little church in a place called Resthaven and we all went there every Sunday. We had Sunday school and I loved going there.

I soon made new friends at Sunday school and all of us went to a government school. It was far away but we had no choice it was the only school available. Sometimes my uncle used to drive us to school in his truck. Unlike our father, my uncle allowed us to get into his car. If he was too busy to drive us he would give us the money for bus fare.

I liked my teacher and I did well in my lessons because I did not want to disappoint him and also, my uncle was interested in my school work. My mum was ok with me but she was hardly around, when she was around she was busy catching up with washing.

My brother who was working at the mines got married and his wife came to live with us and moved into my room. It was ok because I liked her and she helped me with housework. Josie had left by this time and I didn't know why but I had seen her sleeping with one of my cousins in my bed. My cousin said I should not tell anyone but I think I told my uncle. Josie's going did not change anything because she never did much work anyway. My grandmother came to stay as well so we were about 21 of us in that house. There was plenty of food and there were always people from church walking in and out as they pleased, it was really nice.

At school I had lots of friends because I always had money and food from our farm. Sometimes my uncle would give us a lift and for me that was the best life ever, I was really happy. There were lots of fruit trees on the farm and I would climb all of them, I knew where to find the ripe fruits. It was a nice place and I was in heaven, life was wonderful and I had the best Christmas. We actually had new clothes from the shops, not something that my mother made, oh! And my first pair of shoes .We went to church for the Christmas Eve, everybody brought something to share and there was lots of good food.

We celebrated the New Year and went back to school. It was in the middle of the year when all hell broke loose. I came home from school one day to find a truck parked on our driveway and everyone was waiting for me because we had to move, the farm was taken over by the bank. Unfortunately, my dad and my uncle had borrowed money from the bank to start a mining business and it wasn't a success so they were unable to repay the loan. My uncle always had lots of business ideas which never came to pass.

We moved to Resthaven near the church. On the compound where the church was located there were nice cottages, booking rooms, conference and training facilities. We moved into one of the cottages called Hebron and stayed there for a while. Then my mum got a company house at the clinic were she was working and the whole family moved there. It was a step back from the life on the farm, because this was just a block of rooms with no character, no electricity and we had to use public toilets. There was no water in the house so we had to go fetch water from a public tap which was a block away. I was not happy at all there and it was a longer distance to and from school. I lost most of my friends because we were poor again and no one wanted to play with me.

By this time, one of my brothers had finished High school and had got a job with Zimbank as a bank teller. My uncle moved away and because of that I did not have any money and food was scarce, so were friends. At least I still had my teacher who wanted me to get results but even that changed when he was promoted to be a deputy headmaster at a new school and moved away.

I wore my shoes out because of the long walk to school each day and then had to go without shoes for two years because there was no money to buy anything other than food .My mum was transferred to a big government farm and we all had to move with her. Things were really tough because my mum was the only one providing for the family and my brother was drinking a lot so he was not much help to my mum. The company gave her a three-roomed house with no electricity, we had to build a makeshift kitchen of plastic for cooking, and a makeshift toilet- come-bathroom made of grass.

CHAPTER 3

Our family number dropped from twenty one to about twelve because my grandmother died, my brother's wife divorced him and went back to her family and they moved to Malawi with my niece Patricia, we never saw her again. One of my cousins who was my uncle's son and who was much older than me started to abuse me. Whenever I was home alone he would come in and touch me inappropriately and then tell me it was my fault as it was me who as making him do it.

He said if I told anyone he would beat me to death and I believed him because he had a way of finding me home alone. I was so scared of him. When I was 14 the abuse changed and this time he would rub himself against me until he had satisfied himself. He smelled just like the family member who abused me when I was six years old. Although he never really penetrated it was just disgusting that he would do that and his breath was foul. I used to just be limp and go into a trance and start pretending I was in another world where know one would hurt me.

This went on for a long time, sometimes he went away to live somewhere else then he would come back and it would start again. Sometimes he would tell me he was doing that to prepare me and that he actually loved me. There was a time when I nearly told my mum, but menacing threats was all I could think of. He had also said no one would believe me because I was a trouble maker.

One good thing was that I had transferred to a new government school closer to home and I was a senior student. My mum even bought me a pair of shoes but as usual, something had to go wrong. I started getting sick all the time, my mum took me to a hospital to see a specialist and she was told my heart was smaller than my body. This is why I was always getting tired and it got to the stage that I could not even walk and I had to be hospitalized.

I liked the hospital because my cousin would never touch me there, it was my little haven. They had very nice food, a television and lots of books and also, I did not have to do any house work. For a long time I was in a wheelchair because I could not walk at all, I used to feel as if I had no legs. My mum told me I was going to have my heart changed for a bigger one and that got me really scared I was on strong medication and I remember that I used to have about four injections every day.

One of the male nurses started touching me inappropriately. It was starting all over again. He used to bathe me and although I was not yet developed he started to behave just like those who had abused me before so, the hospital was no longer a safe place for me. I then started to believe that it was my fault and that there was something in me that was encouraging these people to behave in that way towards me. I started to think I was different from other girls my age. Eventually I got better and was discharged from hospital but I still had to go back every month for injections and checkups. I started to pray that my heart would just get normal again.

By this time I was in high school and my mum sacrificed for me to go to a private school. She managed to convince my brother who was working at the bank, to pay my school fees. My brother and I were really close so he agreed and I used to wash his clothes for him. Then one day my mum took me to a church and there was this visiting preacher who prayed for me and God healed me. I went back to the hospital for x-rays and my heart was back to normal.

Doctors had told me that if I got pregnant before I was twenty one I would die, but at the age of eighteen I got pregnant and gave birth to my daughter. I had finished my O levels at 17 and I did not really pass, my grades were very low and because of that I could not get a good job, so I sort of hung around at home. I still had to go to the hospital every month for my injections. It was on one of these trips that I met the guy who later raped me. He was a good looking guy and he was a student at a local building college. I cannot say we dated because all he ever did was walk me home whenever he saw me on the road or at the shop.

I can say I liked the attention he gave me but I was afraid to let him get close to me because I did not know how to handle him and also I was scared he would hurt me. I was never alone with him, in fact every time I was along with a guy I just ended up in trouble with my parents. His name was Tanis and he always asked me to his place but I always said 'no' because I was scared .One day I was coming from church when I met Tanis and he walked me home as usual, but this time I was late getting home. My older brother was angry with me and he chased me from the house, neither of my parents were at home so he was left in charge. I had nowhere to go and my little brother had seen that I was thrown out so he walked with me to Tanis house.

When I got to Tanis and told him what had happened, he said we should go and talk in his bedroom and we left my little brother in the other room. Little did I know what was waiting for me in that room, there was no talking. He just forced himself on me, biting me, slapping me and calling me names. I could not scream because my little brother was in the other room and I was scared that this guy would hurt him too. He raped me and chased me out of his house. My brother did not understand what had happened and I could not tell him what had taken place in the bedroom, all I could think of was to go home and find a way to apologize to my older brother and beg him to allow me back into the house. I was in pain but that was the least of my problems, all I wanted was to be allowed back home, if only my mother was there all this would never have happened.

CHAPTER 4

In 1992 my parents bought a small piece of land in a village called Domboshawa and my dad was now living there and building the house. My mum used to go there every weekend, that's why my brother was left in charge. When I got home I was so lucky because my mum was there, she was angry with me for being late but she was even more angry with my brother for chasing me away from home. I was allowed back into the house but I could not tell anyone what had happened to me. I was afraid everyone would say that I had asked for it and those names he called me kept coming back in my mind .One thing I was sure of was that I never wanted to see Tanis ever again.

I knew I was pregnant the first month, but there was no way I was going to live with Tanis. In our tradition, if my parents found out I was pregnant they would have taken me to the person responsible, even if it was against my wish. At first I thought this was the end of my life, I didn't have a job and I never wanted to see the father of the baby that I was carrying. What a dilemma. I was also worried that if my mother found out what had happened, that she would ask me to go and live with Tanis. I had to come up with a plan, I asked my mum if I could go to live with an aunt in another town and my mum thought it was a good idea. Of course, she did not know that I was pregnant.

I stayed with my aunt for four months and it was my aunt who discovered that I was pregnant so she sent me back home. My mum asked me who the father was and I lied to her and said it was someone I had met while living with my aunt. We went back to my aunt's and my mum made a fuss because she wanted the guy's address. I took her to a wrong house and she made a fuss there and she thought that family was covering up. So she took me back home and said we can do without a father. Wow! My plan worked and I was going to have my baby.

My mum helped me to get a job on the farm where we lived. It was not the best of jobs especially for a teenager that was five months pregnant, but it's what I could get and heaven knows we needed the money. So I worked in the field for some time until I was asked to cover for a lady who was on maternity leave and I took her job working in the kiosk. I worked there until the night I gave birth to my beautiful daughter. She was the most beautiful, pretty little baby I have ever seen and I made a vow that I would make sure that she was happy, protected and that she would never starve or go through what I went through. So, two weeks after she was born I went back to work on the farm, and my cousin on my mum's side baby sat for me.

I worked on that farm for a couple months then I got a job at another farm nearby, where we grow flowers in a greenhouse. It was a much better job and I really liked working there. After a year the owners of the farm moved me to their bigger farm and I became a supervisor. My daughter grew and Tanis had moved to another area but somehow he heard that I had a baby, so he came back and tried to make trouble. Finally I had to tell mum what had really happened, she was not happy that I did not trust her with the truth and she threatened to take him to the police if he ever dared to show up again.

I settled at this job, but as usual something bad had to happen. One day I was coming back from work when this man who worked with my mum gave me a lift, he was known for being a lady's man. He was a bit older and he lived with his cousins. I knew him and his reputation but that day transport was a problem, so I was grateful for his lift. Instead of going home he insisted on going through some shops and because I had no other choice I went along with him. Again I was late home and this time, it was not my brother but my father who chased me with an axe. I was determined not to make the same mistake so I went back to the car and we drove around for some time, hoping that if I went home a little later my dad would be asleep and I could sneak into the house.

When I came back my dad was still outside with his axe, he chased me away and this time there was no negotiation because this was my dad who was chasing me and his word was final. So I went with that man to his house. At first this man didn't want to have anything to do with me. However, after a couple of days he went to the local chief and reported that my parents were forcing their daughter on him, so my parents were taken to a civil court. The local chief decided that since I had stayed with him for a couple of days, it was not possible to determine whether or not the man had taken advantage of me, so the man was told to pay my parents some form of compensation. When he realized he had to pay my family he decided he wasn't going to pay for something that hadn't happened, so he started sleeping with me. I became his girlfriend and he was not as bad as my past experiences. Gift, this was his name, worked as a workshop manager at the same farm as my mum.

We lived together for a couple of months and I was still working as a supervisor on the big farm. My mum used to bring my daughter to her work place and I would see her there, she was now two years old. I thought I was going to get married to Gift but that was wishful thinking. One weekend he decided to go on a business trip to another government farm. Well that weekend after he had gone I decided to go visit my mum. It was a Saturday, the day when mum usually brought my daughter with her, so I brought a present for her. I was busy catching up with all the stories from home when Gift's friend came into the clinic to tell me that Gift's wife had come from Bulawayo, another city, where she and Gift were happily married and had a daughter.

My hopes of getting married to a manager disappeared. My dad had gone back to the village by this time so my mum said I should come back home. I did not really love this man so I was glad that I could go back home and be with my daughter. I moved back and I was hoping that maybe Gift would come and explain himself or say sorry but he didn't, he transferred to another farm and I never saw him again for a long time. That was a pity because I was pregnant.

Well I still had my job, so I worked there until they found out I was pregnant. As I was working with chemicals and pesticides, they decided that they could not employ me any longer in my condition. At that same time my older brother who was a big help in our family and had been the one that had paid my school fees, was diagnosed with HIV and Aids and he was dying. So, he came to live with us because the hospitals could not help him, they told him there was no hope for him and he died a month later. He left behind a pregnant girlfriend. His death was a big blow to everyone in the family because he was the only one who had a good job. My other brothers had all grown and moved out. One was working in the mines in Kadoma and lived there with my uncle and his family. My other brothers were living in Kariba and although they had good jobs, they hardly ever visited so it was just me, my little brother, little sister and my daughter left at home.

CHAPTER 5

I gave birth to my son and now I had two children. I had no job, no husband and no longer had my brother to help me because he had just died .It was only my mum that was working and she had so many responsibilities to deal with, including having to pay for my younger sister's education. When my son was a year old I got a job. One of my sister's teachers had a grocery store in a high density suburb in Harare and he was always on the lookout for pretty girls to work in his shops. Of course I had to sleep with him to keep the job but I couldn't tell anyone about it, those were his rules. I later realized that he was sleeping with all the other girls there at different times, while he was 'happily' married.

I worked as a shop assistant, and he got me a place to stay in that area which he paid for and I could live there with my kids. We used to get food in the shop as long as we wrote down in the book what we had taken. I don't remember getting a salary at all because whenever I needed money he would just give it to me.

I really enjoyed the job because it was educationally challenging and I ended up being the buyer. However, I wasn't happy with all the sleeping around that was going on. As a buyer I got to meet a lot of people and I made good friends. As a result, one of my friends offered me a job as a Sales Representative with a big company called Nemchem in an industrial estate in Msasa in Harare. That I can say was moving to greener pastures, I made the biggest sale in two weeks of joining this new company and they employed me without my having to sleep with anyone.

This was a very big organization with so many prospects, I made friends mostly buyers from large companies and I was being invited to lunch in beautiful places, taken to nice hotels for dinner, meeting and hanging around with educated people. I also met people from my high school and we started going out. They taught me to drink alcohol and we went out to night clubs. One of the guys I met was someone I had a crush on when I was at school, he worked for his father and they had a warehouse near where I worked. I fell in love with this guy and actually I think he also loved me. Sometimes he would take me to his family's home in a very nice suburb near were my school was in Vainona. He would wait for me at work and we would go out together, mainly to a bar were we would wait for all his friends to finish work. From there we would go to the Zimbank sports club to drink until they closed and then we'd go to one of his friend's bottle store. With these friends, I got into the habit of drinking.

My work as a sales representative took me across the whole country, selling industrial cleaning equipment and chemicals. My mum thought it would be a good idea if the kids were with her when I travelled out of town so I decided to move back home to live with my mum. I took so much to drinking alcohol that I drank every day.

CHAPTER 6

After two years I found myself pregnant and I tried to talk to my boyfriend but, though he was older than me, he was still immature and loved his drink and partying. He just wasn't ready to be a father, not just to this baby that I was carrying but to my two other kids. It was a hard decision but I had to break up with him without even telling him I was having his child. It was even harder for me but at that time a lot depended on me, my daughter by then was going to school and I needed money for food, for her school fees, bus fare and also having to buy food for everyone at home.

I tried to have an abortion and it didn't work. I lost my job because of all the drinking I was doing. My sales became few and my concentration was shifted because of all that was happening, I was so stressed and depressed. I lost a lot of clients so I got fired, I started to sleep around.

I slept with one of my best friends so I could lie to him and say the pregnancy was his. I went to this other guy who had a good job, but it didn't work out because he was too much into himself. The fact that my little sister was pregnant didn't help because she also had no boyfriend at the time. Her daughter was born in December 1998. I gave birth to another son in 1999.

I spoke to my sister and she agreed to look after both our kids while I went to work. I got a job as funeral insurance broker and it was hard selling, mainly because most of the other girls I worked with were really good at this job and they used to dress very well in their business suits while I had my hand-me-downs.

I remember one day we were in a meeting and my boss was talking about monthly targets. He wanted to give an example so he called me and another girl to the front. She used to top the monthly targets every month she was very well-dressed in her business suits while I wore my hand-me-down clothes that were 4 sizes bigger than me. People started laughing at me and picking on my clothes and that was so humiliating. I blamed myself because when I had money I never thought of buying business suits or other decent clothes, all I ever bought was night club clothes which were not decent enough to wear during the day. That taught me a lesson. I made a vow to myself that I was going to make something of my life that my kids would be proud of and prepare a future for them that they wouldn't have anyone laughing at them.

I began to work hard and I got another job in a pub so I was doing two jobs at the same time. It was very hard because by the time the pub closed there were no busses to go home and the police were arresting any girl they saw walking around in the night. I wasn't the only one with this problem there were other girls as well. I spoke to a receptionist I knew from a hotel I used to frequent when I was hanging around with my friends from school, he agreed to let me sit in the reception of that hotel until morning with the other girls. This happened for a few months.

One day as I was sitting there and my friends were trying to catch some sleep a nicely dressed short man with a large nose called me to the lift, he was obviously booked at that hotel. I was tired and I needed a decent sleep on a bed so much that I just left my friends there and went up to his room with him. I was disappointed when I got there to find he was sharing his room with a friend who had a girl in the room. Well my hope of a good night sleep was dashed and I was about to excuse myself and go back downstairs when the girl whispered that the guys had lots of money and they had just paid her 200 US dollars .

Never in my dreams have I ever 'earned' such money in 30 minutes. Well I got more money than the other girl because the man who had invited me up to his room asked me what I was doing sitting in Reception. I told him we were coming from work and we had to sleep there until day time. He felt so sorry for me that he bought me some drinks and he started asking me a lot about my life. He went down and gave the other girls money for taxis to go home. We talked a lot he told me I was brave and he was impressed by the way I was working hard to support my children. This man gave me 500 US dollars cash and a lot of money in Zimbabwean dollars for my taxi fare. I have never been that happy.

I saw him the day before he left for Malawi, he suggested that I should rent a flat in town near the pub were I worked and he would pay for all the rent and he even bought all the furniture for the flat. Every month he was sending me 1000 US dollars, my daughter was going to school and I was unable to stay with the kids because I was working two jobs and I was never at home. My Mum thought it was a good idea if the kids stayed with her so I saw them every other day and got a girl to help my sister with the children. Life was a bit better, I had a boy friend in Malawi who I only saw twice but he was dedicated to helping me and my kids.

I started sharing a flat with this girl that worked in town and she had a good job there. She could not believe my luck that I could meet someone twice and they could keep paying my rent. This girl and I became really good friends or at least I thought so but little did I know that she was jealous. It was 5 months after I moved in with her that my boyfriend stopped calling me or taking my calls, I called him from a different phone one day and he told me that my room mate had called him to ask him to get me out of her flat because I was bringing in different men, which of cause was not true, but he did not believe me so that was the end of our relationship.

At first I was hurt and devastated because I thought I was in love with this guy and I had so much respect for him. He was different from a lot of guys I had met, he was kind and very gentle and caring, he would actually want to know everything about me and never judged me and not forgetting his generosity as he would send me a 1000 US dollars every month, there is no way I could have cheated on him.

I took to drinking now big time. I drank because I could not sleep, sometimes I did not even have the money to drink but I would go to the night club and I would use any means just to get drunk. There I was angry with my former roommate, I was angry with life, I was bitter and

I didn't care. Apart from tips, I wasn't receiving any pay because my boss at the night club used to find me drinking and because this was against the rules, he wouldn't pay me and sometimes suspended me. At other times he would find me drinking with the customers and in the end he fired me. My attitude was really bad and I even stopped going to the day job with the Insurance Company and in the end they fired me too.

I then had no money to pay my rent at the flat so I went into the streets to look for men who would pay for sex. It was dangerous because the police were always there, so I hooked up with some girls who were into using men to get money. We would do anything to get money. It was prostitution but on a different level where a friend would ask her boyfriend to bring his friends to the house and things would just move on from there. We did not have to be on the streets. The girls and I moved into this one bedroom behind someone's house, we were six girls in that room and we were a total nightmare. We fought with people in night clubs, we stole from men who took us to their houses, and we double crossed guys and never cared. If a man took us to his house and he didn't pay we used take anything we could put our hands on and I remember my friend taking this guy's shoes because he refused to pay her.

It wasn't always easy because sometimes we came across some creeps who had weird fantasies. So we smoked marijuana to make us brave, and sometimes we sold it. We became so well known in the night clubs of Harare and our targets were mainly rich men young or old. Some days were good, some days were bad, it now became like a hobby and we just had to go to the club. It became our source of income and if my mum called to say she didn't have money for food I would go to the club. In the main, we would persuade the bar man to give us water or orange juice, making it look like alcohol and then when someone offered to buy us drinks, we'd asked for expensive drinks and the barman would charge them for the drink. He didn't give us the drink and he didn't put the money in the till but later we would share the profit with him. On a good day we managed to make enough money even for us to lay back and really enjoy and have a good drink and then we didn't have to sleep with anyone.

CHAPTER 7

It was on one of the bad days when the clubs were quiet and nobody was offering to buy drinks. I really needed money for my daughter's school fees and I didn't even have money for taxi to go home. I decided to hike on the main road to my parents' house when this beautiful car stopped and the guy asked me where I was going and I told him. I was in that whatever mood so when he asked me where I was coming from I just told him from the club and that I had been looking for men to pay for sex. He started laughing though I didn't find anything funny and I started explaining to him how times were hard and I was wondering how I was supposed to survive with three children.

He looked at me and asked which school I had gone to because my English seemed perfect to him. I told him and he started asking what went wrong, how I ended up in that profession. I started telling him everything but I don't know why I was being so truthful to him. He asked me what in my ideal world would I want to do and I told him how I wanted so much to go to Malawi to look for my ex boy friend and to explain myself so that maybe he would take me back. To my amazement he reached behind and took out a bag and from that he handed me a wad of money. All in all it was about 500 US dollars, I could not believe my eyes.

He drove me home to my mum's house and I couldn't wait to get out of his car, because I was scared he would change his mind and take the money back. As I was getting out of the car he asked me if I could do a favour for him, he asked me to go get some big orders for him anything as long as it was big. He told me that if I was successful with the orders, I could have a job with his company in Harare. Oh my God not only was I given a life line I was also given a job, I was so happy I ran into the house, packed my bags gave my mum some money and left for Malawi.

Going to Malawi you had to pass though Mozambique and you needed a transit visa just to pass through, I bought the visa on the border and I was off. I got to Lilongwe and called my ex boyfriend but he didn't pick up the phone. I called his friend and told him I was in Lilongwe but the friend came to see me alone and he told me that Charles never wanted to see me again, I was gutted.

I went to Blantyre and booked myself in a hotel and started looking for orders for goods to sell. I made good contacts and forwarded them to my new boss who was then very impressed. I came back from Blantyre to Harare to start my new job as a Research Assistant for this company.

CHAPTER 8

My boss was such a good person and very rich. After a while I started sleeping with him so I had enough money to look after my children, I didn't feel bad about what I was doing, I was just happy someone was paying for the services. I had been done wrong for so long, so used for nothing, abused, beaten up for no reason that I soon became the abuser. I just didn't care whether I hurt anybody in the process; I myself was too broken to care. There were guys I met in that time who actually loved me and cared for me but I just broke their hearts, stole people's husbands then just left them hurt and confused, I broke up so many homes during that time.

I didn't want anyone to get close to me, I was scared if I let someone close they would hurt me, gone was the victim of circumstances and in came this beast that was heartless and care free. Back home things were improving for my children, I had money for food for them and we were now living in a high density location called Hatcliffe where my mum had got me a house through a housing scheme that the government had introduced.

I was still drinking alcohol and clubbing and doing all sorts of sleeping around, I never took life seriously. I met this white guy Herbert, who was out with my friend at this other hotel, we drank a lot that night and we ended up at this other hotel, all three of us in one bed, I don't know how we got there. My friend asked this guy for money the following morning which he gave her and so she left. I was in too much of a hurry to go home and change and go to work that I didn't even ask this guy for money. All I wanted was to go, so he became interested in me because I did not want his money. He gave me a lift and started asking me a lot about myself, but I was not interested, I did not care about him or anyone for that matter. If I wanted money I would just call my boss or he would call and ask if I needed any, the only thing was I was not to tell anyone I was sleeping with him. So I wouldn't say he was my boyfriend, we just slept together and he would give me a lot of money, sometimes he just gave me money without me sleeping with him. I liked this arrangement because they were no strings attached. He had about two wives that I knew about and lots of girlfriends, he was quite rich and he had lived in America for a while.

Sometimes my boss used to book me a hotel for a week and he would just come there once and I would call my friends and we would hang around. My friends and I went on holidays like we were tourists. There was a time we went to a place called Victoria Falls, we got ourselves jobs there as waitresses and it was really good for a while. My friends and I was at our best, our boss the owner of the night club where we were working was paying for our lodgings and used to take us for drinks and introduce us to his friends. We ended up staying there for two months until we got into trouble as this guy was going to beat us up for spending his money and then refusing to sleep with him.

I was choosing the people I was sleeping with at this time because I was not desperate for money. My boss used to call and ask me if I needed any money and if I did he would put it into my bank account. If my mum needed any money for the kids he would drive to Hatcliffe to give it to her. I actually liked him but I could not get serious with him because of his marital status. After the scare in Victoria Falls my friends and I decided to keep a low profile because we were scared of getting beaten up.

I called Herbert who I had met earlier in the year and found out that he was also trying to contact me. We met up for drinks and then we started going out. He was much older and he had a bit of money and lots of time for me. At first we did not understand each other and we argued a lot so I would always call my boss to come and collect me. Somehow he and my boss knew each other and on one of the occasions when my boss came to pick me up after an argument, they ended having a conversation and my boss was not happy that I told of my affair with him. The deal was that I did not to talk to anyone about us so I lost my boss and my job.

CHAPTER 9

In spite of our arguments Herbert was quite serious about me, we started hanging around each other more and he started taking me to his house. I moved back to live with my parents because he didn't like my friends and after a year he asked me to move into one of his flats in town with my children. Life was so much better I was finally with my children and they were going to good schools. He and I travelled a lot in the region and while we were away, I arranged for a lady to come and live at the house to look after the children. My children were actually happy.

I still drank, actually we both drank a lot and we had quite a lot in common. I realized I loved reading so we used to go to the library to get books, then while he was working I would read. In the evening after he finished work he would pick me up from the flat and take me to his house where we would read and have a drink almost every night. I enjoyed spending time at his house and I liked the little bar he had in the house. We would spend time just sitting by the fire, reading or drinking or just talking. He was so knowledgeable about a lot of things, he was mature, educated and I can say I learned a lot from him.

He also had a place in Zambia that he and I would visit often, this life was ok for me for a while but I started to become restless because even though he was rich I didn't have any money of my own. I had a bank account but there was no money in it, if I wanted anything he would just pay for it. He was giving me an allowance but it wasn't much and didn't my bills. I began to worry that if we broke up I would have nothing of my own and I would have to start all over again. All that I had was his.

We started having arguments when I asked him for money to start my own business, he didn't see why I was not happy with him just looking after me. I realized that this was his way of controlling me, he probably thought as long as I was financially dependent on him I wouldn't leave him. Then he threatened that if I leave him he would kill himself. He started to work from home and wanted me to be around him all the time, life with him was becoming suffocating.

I needed to make something of myself and at the same time I really cared for Herbert. He had asked me to marry him several times but each time he was drunk and would change his mind in the morning when he was sober. One day in front of his friends he asked again and I agreed to marry him. Herbert and I travelled to Poland to visit his family and that was my first visit to Europe. I really enjoyed this holiday, it was a good trip and we passed through the UK and did some shopping at Harrods which I loved.

When we got back to Zimbabwe, Herbert gave me some money to start a business but I had to use it to help my brother Davis and his family after he got into some difficulties. Davis and his family then came to live at my house in Hatcliffe while he got himself back on his feet. After a while one of his friends asked Davis to house-sit for him and he and the family moved to a large house in Borrowdale.

Herbert gave me some more money and I decided to go into business with Davis as his business proposal sounded very good but Davis played me. I lost all of the money and while he promised to pay me back, he paid a little at a time and never repaid the full amount.

Herbert got fed up with it all and he ended the relationship. My worst fears came to reality; I was back to square one after five years of us being together. I was lost and got a bit depressed but I had to find a way to go on. I didn't want my children to go back to where we were so I tried going back onto the streets but it was a new breed of young girls in the clubs and I was too old to catch up.

CHAPTER 10

I got myself a lawyer and I sued Herbert for a breach of promise to marry and we ended up with an out-of-court settlement. The agreement was that he would facilitate a visa for me to come to the UK and then provide for my kids for one year. I got the visa and he bought me a ticket to come over to the UK. I arrived and went to live with a friend in Derby. She was one of the girls I used to hang around with in the night clubs in Harare and I had also worked with her at the pub when I had two jobs. She had moved to the UK after the trouble we had got into in Victoria Falls.

I realized when I got here that it was not easy to get a job because I had come on a Visitor's visa, so I babysat for her as she had a daughter. We were really good together she didn't ask me for money for food and rent, she just took me in which was really nice of her. She introduced me to her boyfriend's brother and I started going out with him. He was really sweet and I think he was a virgin when I met him. He started giving me money to send to my children at home. My friend also introduced me to her other boyfriend's mate and I started going out with him as well. He was a nice person but he was in another relationship with someone else. In addition to the two men that I was already seeing, I also met a guy from Turkey who drove a nice car and was really keen on me. It was just like back home where we would date a lot of guys in one go and we never really cared.

I went to Northampton one night to a friend's party when I met this sweet young man named Calvin. He was smoking marijuana outside the house when my friend and I first saw him so we went to ask him for some. One thing led to another and I started dancing with him. I got really drunk and when I woke up I had invited Calvin to our house in Derby. Gosh, I could not remember much of that night. I started talking to him and he stayed over for the whole weekend. I thought it was going to just end there but he called me after a couple of days and told me he wanted to see me again. We had had a good time and in a way I had really enjoyed my time with him. His English was very poor but he was sweet. He started to come over every weekend from Northampton to Derby to see me and I found myself missing him a lot. After that weekend I decided not to sleep with anyone else. I was always thinking of him while I saw the other guys so I decided to end those relationships and I could not wait for him to visit.

One day after spending a lovely day together, Calvin told me he was falling in love with me, and I told him I was feeling the same. I told him about my life and my relationships and that I had dropped all the guys I had been seeing just to be with him. For me that was a big deal because the guys I was breaking up with had money, they were very generous and they were giving me money to send home to my children. Calvin was young and he had nothing. In telling him about my life, I explained that I had three kids and no job and the men I had been sleeping with were giving me money to send back home to support my kids.

I told Calvin about the arrangement I had with Herbert back in Zimbabwe but he never seemed to care about my past, he just asked me one sweet question, whether I had time for him in my future. I knew then that this was the man for me. Me, Stabiso was in love not for money but I was willing to spend the rest of my life with this guy. When I found out I was pregnant with Calvin's child I thought this was it and that he was going to break up with me. Instead, he told me he suspected it and he went and bought a pregnancy-test kit - it was positive, I was going to have another baby.

I felt pity for Calvin because I had a lot on my shoulders but he was so good and understanding about the whole thing. The following week he asked me to marry him and I said a big "yes". The first sober man to go down on one knee and ask me for a hand in marriage, I was so excited and touched. Herbert only used to ask me to marry him whenever he was drunk and then he would change his mind in the morning. I think Herbert asked me more than four times while he was drunk and the final time he asked he was still slightly drunk but there were witnesses on that occasion.

Calvin and I got engaged, we couldn't afford a party but that was ok. I moved from Derby to Northampton to live with him and we were renting a room in someone's house because that's all we could afford at that time.

CHAPTER 11

"Stabiso I am afraid I have some bad news for you" the midwife said as I settled my 7 months old pregnant body on the chair. I wondered what the matter could be. Was something wrong with the baby? My third child was a breach before he was born. I was about to tell the midwife about my son Brian when she said, "Your blood results have come back and I am afraid to tell you that you are HIV positive."

I just closed my eyes and all I could see were the images of my two late brothers Farai and Bongani who died of Aids. I was there when they suffered and died in Africa and to think I was going to suffer the same fate. What about my children in Zimbabwe, my unborn child, my fiancé? All this came into my mind at once and I watched as my world tumbled down. For the first time in my life I was happy and in love. I saw all that happiness disappearing in front of me. The midwife had to shake me to bring me back to reality. She asked if I was ok and I was lost for words. For a loud mouth like me that was a first.

She told me that I was not going to die and that this was not the end of my life. She referred me to the HIV clinic in Northants general Hospital, where she had already booked an appointment for me, for that same day. She explained to me that I had to start taking medication to save my baby and myself and she also told me that there was a chance that my baby would not be affected. I had to have a 'C' section so that my daughter would not be affected and the doctors said that I was not to breast feed. I gave birth to a beautiful baby girl in February of 2006.

Calvin had been ok with the HIV news; he didn't break up with me and supported me through all the process of starting medication and attending counseling sessions with me. He and our daughter were also tested and both were negative.

Calvin was the only one working at the time and I was at home with the baby. Although I had stopped drinking once I knew I was pregnant, after the baby was born I started drinking again because I was angry with the situation and confused. Sometimes I used to leave Calvin with the baby and go clubbing at night. Calvin didn't mind me drinking but sometimes we were so broke because he also had to help me with money to send home to my kids in Zimbabwe.

I was happy being with Calvin but I was angry about the HIV and drinking seemed to be the only thing that brought comfort. Once I started drinking I would end up at the club. I felt carefree, danced, got wasted, got home and slept but when I awoke, I had a hangover, was filled with regret and had a baby to look after. Being broke was the only thing that stopped me from drinking and clubbing.

CHAPTER 12

One night while we were sleeping I had a dream, and in that dream I heard a voice saying to me "I am the Lord your God and I want you to acknowledge Me for all the good things happening in your life." I looked around and there was no one in the room. I awoke Calvin and he hadn't heard anything so went back to sleep. The room felt like there was a presence in there, you know, like when you switch off a television there is a light that lingers on it, it was like that. I couldn't shake it off, that voice kept coming back to me. I took my diary and wrote down every word and I then took my phone and went downstairs and called my sister-in-law who was a Christian and lived in Nottingham. She said it was about time I got saved and I told her I didn't know how to pray. She said I should just say "thank you" and she also said I should look for a church near me. I went back to bed and said "Thank you

Lord" but in my heart I knew that was not enough, that voice kept coming back to me.

The following day I was looking through the post and I saw a pamphlet from a church called Northampton Deliverance church. I called the number and they came to pick me up that Sunday, I hadn't been in a church for a long time since I was in my twenties. After I'd had to two kids and wasn't married my mum had tried her best to take me to church in a hope that I would probably get a decent guy to marry me.

The first thing I noticed and liked when I got to church was the music it was really good and not boring. After a while a lady went to the front and started speaking in a funny language. She then changed and spoke in the voice and tone like I had in my dream, saying "I am the Lord your God and I want you to acknowledge me for all the good things happening in your life". That was word for word what I had heard in my dream I knew it all because I had written it down in my diary and those words were always on my mind since the dream.

I felt an overwhelming presence in the church that God was there and he was calling me and talking to me. I bawled my way to the front of the church and I gave my life to Jesus. I have never in my life felt like that, I cried my life out all the hurt the pain I was carrying everything, I gave it all to him that day and I left that place light headed and at peace. I never really cried before I was always this carefree spirit who used to find it hard to cry. I remember they were times when I used to go with my friends to smoke weed before we'd go to a funeral so we could just shed some tears.

I had became so heartless that I wouldn't want anyone to see I was hurting inside so mainly I would put on this persona as a tough person and to me, crying was a sign of weakness. I remember there was a time I was talking to my sister-in-law (Davis' wife) and I was telling her about some guy I cared about and that he had broken my heart and she had said to me "but Aunty do you have a heart?". I had cried all my tears as a child whenever I was alone and scared and had been abused, so I grew to just mask my feelings and pretend that whatever was happening was not really happening and I would imagine myself in another world.

I got home a changed person. All of a sudden a lot of things I used care about did not matter any more. I was loved by the Most High God and I was touched to know that He cared for me so much that He called me Himself. I told Calvin that I was saved and I had given my life to Jesus but he did not understand what was going on inside and I think he still doesn't understand.

Nevertheless every day I pray for his salvation as I know that God can save him, if He can save me He can save Calvin. There was a time when I wanted Calvin to change with me, but I have come to trust in the Lord and believe God for his salvation and I continue to love Calvin like Jesus loved me.

God loved me regardless of my mess, He saw through all my façade and reached deep down in my soul and saved me. I was a brand new creation, there was a drastic change in my life and the things I used to hold dear all of a sudden were of no significance. Also there was a peace inside me that I still cannot explain. A month later I got baptized in Jesus' name, there was no going back for me. Jesus was the King and saviour of my life, my redeemer and my provider.

I heard that there was a Ministry-equipping school and I decided to apply for a place and was able to enrol in September 2006. I spoke to Calvin and he agreed to pay the fees for me and to look after our daughter while I was at school.

In the early days of my attendance at the school, I was still finding it difficult to forgive people who had hurt me or to forgive anyone who hurts children. As time passed by, I was learning so much and God gave me the grace to forgive and He delivered me from bitterness. It was good to know that God has called us to be witnesses of His son Jesus Christ even those who hurt us, because without Jesus they will keep hurting people.

At first I was finding it difficult to understand what I was reading in my Bible and putting that into my everyday situation. But by the end of the equipping year we were actually able to prepare and give sermons and arrange missions. The transformation was so evident in my everyday life.

I started to experience God's favour in my personal life, we had been living in a one bedroom house and had applied for a council house but the process seemed to be taking forever. God just started giving us favour in that regard, we got a two bedroom ground floor flat in a brand new block of flats. I had also been struggling to get a permit to reside in the country but by God's grace we went to court and my case was successful and I received my permit.

Soon afterwards, I started applying for my kids to come and join Calvin and me and by God's grace and the help of all my friends in church who were praying to make this possible, I now have all my children with me. God has been faithful in many ways and I can never thank Him enough. He has given me a new family in Christ and a new identity as a child of the Most High God.

CHAPTER 13

Before I got saved I had no direction I was just a drifter but now I have been studying which is something I never thought in my wildest dreams I would do. A friend and I are working on a project to establish a charity in Zimbabwe to support people infected and affected by HIV and Aids. We are working to develop the vision and trust God to make a way for this vision to be fulfilled. My heart cries out to the people of my country who are dying like flies, everyday someone I know is dying of this disease and because of the political and economical situation in Zimbabwe a lot of people cannot afford the necessary medication that can help them sustain a healthy living. I am lucky to be here and it is all because of God's grace, without it I would be dead by now like most of my friends.

This is why I am strongly convinced that God has delivered me from the enemy's destructive plan and has pulled me from the dust bin, set me in the path of restoration and has given me a new identity. I now care not only about myself and my family but about helping other people who are not in a position to help themselves. I have changed from being a carefree person into someone who has a heart for others. He has cleansed me from all unrighteousness and purified me and changed my mentality by His blood. I am now a new creation, behold all things have become new. My bible says He who began a good work in me, He will be faithful to complete it. The Lord is changing me little by little every day it has been a journey and I know by His grace I will become the person He has created me to be.

I would like to thank you for reading this testimony and hope that you will share this book. For those who have not received Christ as their personal saviour, I encourage you to take a minute and invite Jesus Christ into your heart and let him be your Lord and saviour. It only takes a prayer you will find this prayer at the end of this book.

As for me and my family we will serve the Lord.

CONCLUSION

Redemption

The reason why I have chosen to write this book and open up the deepest and darkest parts of my life is because my heart is to reach out to people in my situation or anyone who knows people in the same situation. It is my testimony to show the world that Jesus is real and He can reach down to the lowest, darkest point in your life and turn it around for the good. There is no sin that God cannot forgive.

The choices and the lifestyle I was leading were surely going to take me to destruction. All the drugs, drinking, prostitution, manipulation, adultery, bitterness, hurt, pain, un-forgiveness was leading me towards death and destruction but God in his infinite mercy reached down into my world of doom and gloom and redeemed my soul and set me on a path of salvation, hope and destiny. God can reach down to wherever you are.

A lot of people think their sins are too great for God to forgive them but the Word of God says in Psalm 139 verses 7-8 "Where can I go from your Spirit ?Or where can I flee from your Spirit ?If I ascend into heaven you are there; If I ascend into hell, behold you are there." The bible talks about God sending his son Jesus Christ to die for our sins. He paid the ultimate price for our sins by dying a cruel and painful death on the cross so that we could be set free and be able to have a relationship with God. Redemption

Hope

It does not matter where you come from or what background you come from God can change your tomorrow for the better. God is a god of restoration and a mender of broken lives. My life was full of brokenness but Jesus has made me whole. What the enemy meant for bad and to destroy our lives God can change it for good. Jeremiah 29 v 11 says that "For I know the thoughts that I have towards you says the lord, thoughts of peace and not of evil to give you a future and a hope".

Jesus is still in the business of changing lives of people whom society has labelled as outcasts and rejected because of their lifestyles. There was one such woman in the bible in John chapter 4 from verse 7. We see Jesus speaking to a Samaritan woman at the well and he offered her living waters which is salvation of her soul. She must have been surprised that Jesus would even speak to her. This is because Jews were not allowed to socialise with Samaritans, Jews were seen as more superior to the gentiles and also she was a woman who had a bad reputation as she had 5 men who were not her husband. Jesus knew this but yet he offered her salvation.

Destiny

God has an awesome plan for our lives He uses what was working against us or what the enemy meant for bad for good. God never wastes anything in our lives. Even in our times of darkness or when we seem to be on the wrong path God is there. The bible says He will never leave us nor forsake us. I can look back at my life and see how God spared my life so many times because I was in so many dangerous situations.

God has changed my heart and I have compassion for girls that are on the street and prostitution. My desire is now to use the life experiences I have to establish an organisation to help girls get off the streets and equip them with skills to earn a decent living or start income-generating projects. My other desire is to help people that are infected and affected by HIV and AIDS and start an orphanage in Zimbabwe. I have started working on this project with a friend.

African Tradition and customs

Some of the traditions in Africa work against young girls and women. Forced marriage is one of these customs .This is called "Kutizira "and this happens when a girl is found to be pregnant out of wedlock. She is interrogated by the family to find out who is responsible for getting her pregnant. She is taken without her consent to the man or boy responsible and that person is forced to take her in as his wife.

At times African parents are so strict that if you are late in getting home you are chased away from home and told to go back to where you have come from. This promotes fear within children and there is no platform where children can reason with their parents or speak to them about issues affecting them. In my situation it left me vulnerable where I was left in the hands of people that abused me when I should have been under the safety and protection of my parents.

Parents/Family

Parents need to develop a close and loving relationship with their children. They need to provide an environment where children are free to discuss their concerns or any problems they are facing. Abuse and neglect normally happen in the home. One of the ways to counteract this problem is to develop an honest and open relationship with your children, additionally be aware of any changes in your child. In my own situation I became withdrawn and lived in my own world, no one noticed or questioned me. As I grew I became rebellious and I was judged and labelled but no one took the time to sit down and find out what was going on. They did not find out what had made me rebel against the God they believed in.

Victims of abuse

For anyone reading this book that has been a victim of abuse, I want you to know that whatever went wrong God can make it right. There is hope in your situation God can turn it around. There is a message in every mess, you might not see the light or you may feel that God has forsaken you when you a going through your situation but God is with you. If you find yourself in this situation speak out do not be bound by fear even if the perpetrator is threatening your life. Seek a Christian, someone you trust or Child Line (or any established organisation that deals with matters of abuse), any family member or the police.

Shame/Stigma

There is a lot of shame attached to being abused, being a prostitute or being diagnosed with HIV. Shame is debasing it affects your self esteem, you feel dirty, like an outcast in society and you lack trust in people. The bible says in 2 Corinthians 5 v 17 "Therefore if anyone is in Christ he is a new creation; old things have passed away; behold all things have become new". God can change our story, when you become born again your old ways and mentality can be wiped clean. God can deliver you from all the shame and pain and restore you. You can begin again in God.

Forgiveness/Moving forward

When God begins to restore your life and heal the pain in your heart, it is a process and He will take you on a journey to rebuild your life. In order to move on you need to forgive your abuser; those who let you down and you need forgive yourself. Remember it is not your fault that you were abused.

Forgiveness liberates you and the perpetrator no longer has a hold on you. I chose to forgive and because of that I can freely speak about what happened to me and my past and my abusers have no hold over me. Philippians 3 verse 13 -14 declares that "Brethren, I do not count myself to have apprehended; but one thing I do, forgetting those things which are behind and reaching forward to those things which are ahead. I press toward the goal for the prize of the upward call of God in Christ Jesus".

In order to get hold of your future you need to let go of your past. I am not saying it is any easy journey because sometimes you will have good days and bad days but if you trust in God he will help you get through it.

Salvation

God reached down in the midst of my mess, in my darkest hour and pulled me out by his righteous hand of mercy and turned my life around. He gave me a hope, a future, purpose and direction for my life. I am fully convinced as I am writing this that I am moving forward into my destiny. If you feel that there is no direction in your life and you have been going round in circles there is a way out God is our answer.

If you feel you have sinned so much or you have done a lot of wrong in your life, God can set you free and bring you out of any situation you might find yourself in. The bible says "If you confess with your mouth the Lord Jesus and believe in your heart that God has raised him from the dead you will be saved". (Romans 10 v 9)

If you do not know the Lord as your personal saviour and you desire to see change in your life you can pray the prayer of Salvation below.

PRAYER OF SALVATION

Dear Lord Jesus
I confess that I am a sinner and I believe that you sent your son Jesus Christ to die for my sins. I believe in my heart that he died and rose again on the third day and is sitting on the right hand of the father. I invite you into my heart as my Lord and personal saviour.
In Jesus Name
Amen.

You are saved now and Jesus will now take you on a journey of restoration and destiny. Angels are celebrating your salvation. Hallelujah. The next step is to pray about a bible-based church, fellowship with other Christians and get baptised.

BIOGRAPHY

Stabiso Madziva is a mother of four beautiful children. She is currently residing in Northampton, United Kingdom with her family. She has an evangelistic call on her life and has a hunger to see souls get saved. She has a passion for helping and giving a Voice to the oppressed.

2011